MW01008436

TANGLED IN THE TINSEL

TANGLED IN THE TINSEL

A Look at Christmas Through Sketches
and Monologues for All Ages

by Martha Bolton

Author of *A Funny Thing Happened to Me on My Way
Through the Bible, A View from the Pew,*
and
What's Growing Under Your Bed?

A LILLENAS Drama Resource

Lillenas Publishing Co.
Kansas City, MO 64141

Copyright © 1987 Lillenas Publishing Co.
All rights reserved.

Printed in the United States of America.

No part of these scripts may be reproduced by any method whatsoever, except by the procedure noted below.

You may duplicate individual sketch scripts from this collection for $1.00 per copy—$10.00 maximum per individual script. Please include this statement on each reproduced script:

From *Tangled in the Tinsel*. Copyright © 1987 by Lillenas Publishing Company. All rights reserved. Used by permission.

Permission is granted upon the receipt of your check. Please indicate sources of script(s), title(s), number of copies made, and the performance date(s). Mail your request and check to:

Lillenas Drama Resources
Permission Desk
P.O. Box 419527
Kansas City, MO 64141

Dedication

To my sons
  Rusty, Matt, and Tony
    —who have made the holidays what
    they are today—EXPENSIVE!
      (. . . and a whole lot of fun!)

Contents

Foreword   9

Preface   13

Acknowledgments   15

The Great Parking Space Race   17
A comedy sketch for 1 man and 1 woman

The Holiday Ham   20
A comedy sketch for 3 characters and extras

Visions of Sugarplums (and Other Things Fattening)   23
A comedy sketch for 3 men, 3 women, and extras

The Christmas Scramble   28
A comedy sketch for 14 children

Store Wars   31
A comedy sketch for 2 women and another person

O Blessed Night of Stage Fright   35
A comedy monologue for a boy (or girl)

'Tis Better to Give . . .   37
A comedy sketch for 2 boys and a woman

The Twelve Months of Christmas   42
A comedy sketch with music for 12 singers

Special Delivery   48
A comedy sketch for 3 persons

You're on the Air   51
A comedy sketch for 1 adult and 9 children

Oh, Christmas Tree! Oh, Christmas Tree!   55
    A comedy sketch for 1 man and 1 woman

The Recitation   58
    A comedy sketch for 1 young teen boy, 1 girl, and
    1 woman

The Relative   62
    A comedy sketch for 2 men and 1 woman

The Annual Gift Exchange   68
    A comedy monologue for a woman

Mistletoe Macho   70
    A comedy sketch for 1 man and 3 women

**I'll Be Home for Christmas . . . if I Ever Get Waited
on at the Mall**   73
    A comedy sketch for 2 men, a woman, and extras

The Christmas Feast (or) Eat, Drink, and Get Heartburn   77
    A comedy sketch for 3 men and 2 women

The Birthday Party   80
    A comedy sketch for 9 persons

A Different Christmas   84
    A comedy sketch for 1 man, 2 boys, 1 woman, and 1 girl

Foreword

The scene is an autographing event in either Dallas or Washington, D.C. The occasion is the annual international convention of Christian Booksellers (C.B.A.). The cast of characters include Martha Bolton (successful Lillenas author), fans (long lines of them), and me (representing the publisher and holding open the books that Martha autographs).

At this particular moment, a bookstore dealer from a town in one of the Dakotas is requesting that Martha inscribe her free copy of *A View from the Pew* (or maybe it was *A Funny Thing Happened to Me on My Way Through the Bible*), "To Mable . . ."

LADY *(from one of the Dakotas):* It's "Mable." Spell it M-A-B-L-E, not M-A-B-E-L. And by the way, Miss Bolton, we just love your books. They're *so* funny!

MARTHA *(demurely):* Well, thank you . . .

LADY *(interrupting):* Why I was just telling Fred last week, Fred's my stock boy, it's about time we had another Martha Bolton book around here. And, sure enough, here you are with a brand-new one. Is it funny?

MARTHA *(even more demurely):* Well, I certainly hope . . .

LADY *(continuing):* Yes siree, Fred and I love your books. Oh, could you write one to Fred? He'd just love it. It's "Fred," F-R-E . . .

At the close of that one-hour autographing session (that's 300 books later!) Martha less than demurely questioned, "Do you think the new one's funny?" What a question! Of course it's funny—but better than that, every Bolton book has a reason behind it. While your funny bone is being stroked, your heart says, "Yeah, that's true." People from the Dakotas know that, and so do thousands more all over the world.

It was a red-letter day indeed when Lillenas asked Martha Bolton to consider writing a book of humorous sketches for all kinds of occasions—and she accepted. How did we find her? Well, if I remember correctly, she found us.

As compiler of the various Lillenas Program Builder collections, I ran across an occasional manuscript by one Martha Bolton of Simi, Calif. Without fail, the skit or sketch was a knockout. Each had all the earmarks of an author who was able to put realistic dialogue onto paper, whose writing had a sense of rhythm and timing, who obviously knew the stuff of which she wrote, and sure as anything, had an appreciation for Christian values. In short, she was a bright light in the murky task of reading unsolicited free-lance manuscripts.

"Who are you?" I wrote in a query letter. "Why don't we receive more of your work on a more regular basis? Are you under contract to another publisher?"

In a few days, what would become a familiar No. 10 buff envelope with a Simi, Calif., return was in my mail tray. Inside was a letter and a much-folded full-page newspaper clipping, which I set to one side in favor of the written message.

"Perhaps the enclosed story from our hometown newspaper will explain a bit about me," I read. So I opened the news clipping and what to my wondering eyes should appear, but a full-page story and photos describing Martha Bolton as a committed Christian, the wife of a Los Angeles Police Department officer (Juvenile Division), and mother of three boys. Then the clincher—Martha Bolton is part of the team of five comedy writers who provide the inimitable Bob Hope with his strings of matchless one-liners and quips. The story explained that this is a full-time job that provides Martha with television on-screen credit for every Hope special (she's the first woman writer to have this honor), membership in the exclusive Writers Guild of America, West, and a beeper. The beeper is Hope's summons to get to a telephone for a writing assignment. The call can come directly from him in his dressing room backstage at some national event where he is in need of a batch of last-minute gags to fit a specific situation or fast-breaking news happening, or from the team's head writer.

In a typical workday Martha writes 50 to 100 jokes. Her boss always knows where she is and how she can be reached by phone. At the C.B.A. convention referred to above, the blonde writer, upon her return to the hotel, more than once was met by a desk clerk with the message "Call Bob Hope." Each time she called in, the request was for more jokes on President Reagan's involvement in whatever the hot news item of the day was.

Also included in the article were references to other credits: a humor column for her local newspaper, gags and jokes for comedienne Phyllis Diller and cartoonist Bill Hoest, creator of the "Lockhorns" strip, and her church involvements.

"I cut my teeth as a writer at church," she says. "Whenever there would be a tribute to a member or an anniversary for a pastor or a special skit was needed, I'd write the script. Humor, especially in churches, plays a crucial role in communicating with people. Things that stick in peoples' minds are often humorous. People like to laugh. There are enough sad times for all of us. The happy times hold us over. All in all, I would rather laugh."

So this was Martha Bolton. By return mail I asked her to write a full collection of sketches based on familiar Bible stories. She responded with *A Funny Thing Happened to Me on My Way Through the Bible* (which broke some kind of Lillenas record for title length). A year later she produced *A View from the Pew*—subtitled "From the Potluck to the Bored Meeting"—followed by *What's Growing Under Your Bed?* All of them Lillenas best-sellers.

And now, it's with pleasure and a chuckle that I am able to introduce *Tangled in the Tinsel.* Enjoy these sketches. Read them for fun, stage a few at your next all-church Christmas dinner, and be sure to give copies to *everyone* on your gift list.

It has been an absolute pleasure working with Martha on each of these projects. Her frequent phone calls are always punctuated with laughter and news about her latest writing project. She still types letters on the buff-colored stationery with its smiley mouth and plumed pen. While humor is obviously a high priority in her life, so is her commitment to Christ, which results in an ever-present vision that her entertainment-world contacts are an arena for witness to life in Christ.

—PAUL M. MILLER

Preface

I know. You've been appointed director of the annual Christmas program. You've been made chairman of the youth holiday social. You're in charge of entertainment at the all-church Christmas banquet. In other words, you were absent when the nominations were taking place, and now you're elected.

You've checked the flights out of town. They're booked solid due to holiday travelers. You've checked with AMTRAK and Greyhound. Same story. Now you have to face facts. There's no way out. You've got to come up with a program that's seasonal, entertaining, and simple.

Well, relax. The following 19 sketches and monologues are so easy to produce you'll be volunteering to be entertainment chairman again next year. And the year after, and the year after that. In fact, your church may have to hold a special election just to get you out of the position!

These sketches can be used singularly or in any combination for the program length you desire. There are parts for each age-group, and every aspect of the holiday season has been covered—from learning your part in the Christmas pageant to finding a parking place at the mall.

So, c'mon, cancel your hot air balloon escape out of the country. Putting together your yuletide entertainment is going to be easier than you thought. Your audience will laugh at the frustrations of Christmas while being reminded of the importance of the occasion. And remembering what Christmas is really about is the best way to keep us all from getting tangled in the tinsel.

Have fun, and Merry Christmas!
MARTHA BOLTON

Acknowledgments

To my husband, Russ, for all the times he couldn't get through to me on the telephone. (He claims I talk on it 24 hours a day. But that's not true. Part of the time I'm dialing!)

To Paul Miller and Ken Bible who let me hang around with them at Christian Booksellers Association conventions.

To the ministers who encouraged my early writing career: Revs. Lavonnie (Lee) Ferren, Gene Paul, Carl Burns, Cecil Barham, Irvin Zuehlsdorf, David Sloat, Robert C. Cunningham, D. Leroy Sanders, Thomas Fuller, Duane Weis, Jonathan Harrel, David Skaggs, Frank Edwards, Lloyd Guess, Bill Enos, John McIntosh, John Arnold, and Rich Guerra. (If I failed to mention anyone, they can thank me later.)

The Great Parking Space Race

A Comedy Sketch

Characters:

WILBUR
WILLADENE

Setting:

Two chairs signifying a car (It'd be four, but this is a sportscar.)

Costumes:

Modern-day dress

▽

(Sketch opens with WILBUR *and* WILLADENE *sitting in the car.* WILBUR *is driving, and after many trips around the parking lot, he has finally landed a parking space.* WILLADENE, *however, is not impressed.)*

WILLADENE: Is this the closest you can get to the store?

WILBUR: How much closer do you want?

WILLADENE: Well, it'd be nice if we were in the same zip code.

WILBUR: Can I help it if the store's crowded tonight? We'll just have to park here and walk back.

WILLADENE: I hope you brought a canteen.

WILBUR: Don't be so dramatic. We're not THAT far away.

WILLADENE: Are you kidding? By the time we get to the store, they'll be having their AFTER Christmas sales. *(Pointing)* Hey, wait! Isn't that an empty space over there?

WILBUR: Yeah, but the people in that other car saw it first.

WILLADENE: So? Our car's bigger than theirs.

WILBUR: Shopping brings out the worst in you, doesn't it, Willadene?

WILLADENE: Well, what about over there? *(She points in another direction.)*

WILBUR: Over where?

WILLADENE: By the front of the store. That empty area. There aren't any cars parked there.

WILBUR: Of course not. That's the sidewalk.

WILLADENE: Well, it's not as though we're parking overnight! And besides, the sign just says "No bicycles or skateboards." It doesn't say anything about Chevys.

WILBUR: Shh, wait a minute! Do you see the guy standing by that blue car two aisles over?

WILLADENE: Yeah. What about him?

WILBUR: I think he's stealing it.

WILLADENE: You're kidding!

WILBUR: He looks awfully suspicious.

WILLADENE: Well, see if you can get closer.

WILBUR: Why? To get his description for the police?

WILLADENE: No. To make sure we get his parking space when he pulls out.

WILBUR *(shaking his head)*: You're a cold woman, Willadene.

WILLADENE: Look, when you've done as much shopping as I have over the years, you learn to survive. Anyway, all I want is a decent parking space. Is that too much to ask?

WILBUR: But shouldn't we call the police?

WILLADENE: They've got better things to do than to find us a parking space.

WILBUR: I mean, to report that guy.

WILLADENE: They'd just have to come down here, and then where are THEY going to park? Besides, look, he's walking away.

WILBUR: I guess he figured if he had to give up that great of a parking space, it wasn't worth stealing the car.

WILLADENE: Well, isn't that an empty space over there?

WILBUR: You're right! It is! It's a little tight, but I think we can squeeze in. *(He maneuvers the car into the empty space.)* How am I doing on your side?

WILLADENE: You've got about an inch to spare. Wait! Make that two inches. You just peeled off our side moldings. . . . How 'bout your side?

WILBUR: It's close, but I'm making it. *(He continues maneuvering.)* Yes, yes . . . perfect! OK, now you can get out.

WILLADENE: How? Through the window? I can't even open my door!

WILBUR: You're never satisfied, are you, Willadene? All right, look, this is it. One more trip around this place, and then we're going home. If I don't find a parking space, that's it! It's adios, au revoir, arrivederci, sayonara . . .

WILLADENE: You're giving up that easily?

WILBUR: I have to. There's not that much tread left on the tires.

WILLADENE: Wait! I think I see one! Yes, that's one! Look! *(Points.)* Over there!

WILBUR: Well, I don't believe it! You're right! That *is* an empty parking space . . . and it's right smack in front of the store! This is amazing! After all our driving around in circles, fender-fighting cars over premium spaces, and trying to squeeze into compact parking spots, we finally found one! And it's a beauty at that! Right up here by the store's entrance. We couldn't have asked for a better space! *(He maneuvers the car into the parking space, and turns off the engine.)* This is great! We're so close, this is almost as good as valet parking! *(Starts to get out.)* Well, come on! Get out! We've got Christmas shopping to do!

WILLADENE: Uh, dear . . .

WILBUR: Yes?

WILLADENE: The store just closed.

The Holiday Ham

A Comedy Sketch

Characters:

H. H. (short for HOLIDAY HAM)
WAYNE
DIRECTOR
4 or 5 EXTRAS

Setting:

Stage is set for typical Christmas play rehearsal (i.e., the streets of Bethlehem)

Props:

Scripts

Costumes:

Everyone but Director is dressed in Bible-era costume;
Director is in modern-day dress

▽

(Sketch opens with WAYNE *and* EXTRAS *on stage, scripts in hand, talking amongst themselves.* H. H. *enters, bigger than life.)*

H. H.: All right, cast, this is it. This is the final dress rehearsal on the last day before the big night. Tomorrow's the Christmas play, and from then on it's fame, fans, and fortune. . . . For *me,* that is. (EXTRAS *roll their eyes and continue about their private conversations.)*

WAYNE: Hey, what about me? I've got a part, too, you know.

H. H.: Ah, yes, you're the one who shouts "Hark!" aren't you?

WAYNE *(defensively)*: I've got a bigger part than that!

H. H.: You do?

WAYNE: Yeah. I shout it TWICE!

H. H.: My, my. How did you ever memorize it all?

WAYNE: Look, it may only be two words, but they're IMPORTANT words.

H. H.: Well, OF COURSE they are. They give me a chance to catch my breath between monologues.

WAYNE: You really think you're something, don't you?

H. H.: Only because all the evidence points that way. You see, I've studied, I've rehearsed, and I'm, well, I'm your basic "star" material. What more could a director ask for?

WAYNE: Have you prayed?

H. H.: That's not in the script.

WAYNE: Neither was the operetta you threw in yesterday during the shepherd scene, but that didn't stop you.

H. H.: A little ad lib. Big deal.

WAYNE: Well, don't you think you should be praying for God to bless our performance tomorrow?

H. H.: I've been too busy to pray. I've had to memorize lines and call talent scouts, rehearse my scenes and call talent scouts, get fitted for my costume and call talent scouts.

WAYNE: Just how many talent scouts did you call?

H. H.: Well, actually, only the one, but he kept hanging up on me. Anyway, God understands. He wants my best performance, too, you know. And besides, I'll be talking to Him at the cast party. I'm sure they'll want me to pray over the refreshments or something.

WAYNE: You're right, God does want your best performance. But that means one that comes from your heart.

H. H.: My heart? I didn't see that on the props list.

WAYNE: Probably no one knew you had one. But trust me, it'll be the most important thing you can bring to your performance tomorrow night.

H. H.: You really take this seriously, don't you?

WAYNE (nods): I came to know the Lord during a Christmas play two years ago. . . . In fact, if my memory serves me correctly, you were in that one, too, weren't you?

H. H.: Oh, no. You must be mistaken.

WAYNE: Sure, it was you.

H. H.: Impossible.

WAYNE: No, I remember. You were one of the sheep.

H. H.: Sorry, it wasn't me.

WAYNE: It HAD to be you. It was the only sheep costume with glitter!

H. H.: Just a little around the shoulders . . . for effect.

WAYNE: Well, anyway, the point is that play spoke to my heart, and my life was changed.

H. H.: All because of a Christmas play?

WAYNE: All because of a Christmas play.

H. H. *(thinks for a moment):* Maybe you're right. Maybe I should start looking at this as a ministry instead of my ticket to fame.

(DIRECTOR enters.)

DIRECTOR *(claps hands twice):* Places, everyone, places.

(They all take their proper places on stage.)

WAYNE *(whispers to H. H.):* Just remember, the best performance comes from your heart.

H. H.: All right, but this doesn't mean I have to give up my fan club, does it?

WAYNE: No, he doesn't hurt anything.

DIRECTOR: And action!

H. H. *(in character):* Ah, Bethlehem, how your streets . . . *(Stops suddenly, then looks back at Wayne.)* What do you mean, "he"?

(Blackout.)

Visions of Sugarplums (and Other Things Fattening)

A Comedy Sketch

Characters:

> BOB
> TONY
> LINDA
> Various other CAROLERS
> COUPLE IN HOUSE NO. 1
> LADY IN HOUSE NO. 2

Setting:

> Three free-standing doors to represent three different homes

Props:

> Carolers' songbooks

Costumes:

> Carolers should be dressed warm

▽

(Sketch opens with COUPLE IN HOUSE NO. 1 *standing in doorway listening to* CAROLERS. CAROLERS *are singing ending of "Joy to the World.")*

CAROLERS *(singing together):* And heav'n and nature sing. . . . And heav'n and nature sing. . . . And heav'n and heav'n and nature sing. *(They wave and start walking away.)* Good night! And Merry Christmas!

COUPLE IN HOUSE NO. 1: And a Merry Christmas to you! *(They wave, and close the door. They should now be outside of the view of the audience.)*

BOB: Can you believe that? They didn't even offer us any hot chocolate.

LINDA: You don't go Christmas caroling just to get hot chocolate, do you?

BOB: Of course not. I expect cookies, too.

LINDA: But caroling is something you're supposed to do for the enjoyment of others.

BOB: Well, NATURALLY it's for the enjoyment of others. Do you think *I* enjoy freezing out here?

LINDA: It is a bit chilly, isn't it?

BOB: A bit chilly? Are you kidding? Not only can I see my own breath, but I can make an ice sculpture out of it! Why, it's so cold even the flies are wearing earmuffs.

TONY: Now, where would a fly get earmuffs?

BOB: I don't know. I asked him, but I don't think he could hear me.

TONY: Well, where shall we carol next?

BOB: I vote for McDonalds.

LINDA: C'mon, get serious.

BOB: I am. We can carol our way through the drive-thru. You know, sort of a McDeck the McHalls.

LINDA: Will you PLEASE get your mind off of food and onto sharing the spirit of Christmas with others.

BOB: But the Christmas spirit is just exactly what I want to share. Fruitcake, eggnog, candy canes, Christmas cookies . . .

TONY: Whatever happened to "love, peace, and goodwill toward men"?

BOB: I don't think they're edible.

LINDA: Well, what about that house over there? *(She points to middle door.)*

BOB: It doesn't look edible either.

LINDA: I meant to carol at!

BOB: Yeah, why not? It smells like they're cooking something good.

TONY: All right, but remember, we're just going over there to sing, not place an order.

BOB: OK, but if my stomach starts growling and drowns out the entire alto section, don't say I didn't warn you. *(They walk over to middle door, and ring the doorbell.)*

LINDA: I don't think anyone's home.

BOB: We wouldn't have that problem at McDonalds.

LINDA *(pretending to look in window of middle house)*: Oh, look, isn't that a beautiful little tree in the window?

BOB: Yeah, and what I wouldn't give for a couple of those popcorn strands.

LINDA: You'd eat tree decorations?

BOB: Only when they're in season.

TONY: Hey, I think I see a light.

BOB *(looks heavenward)*: O Lord, please let it be coming from a microwave.

TONY: Well, I say we start singing and if they're home, they'll come on out.

LINDA: OK. Let's start with *(sings)* "Chestnuts roasting . . ."

BOB *(cuts in)*: Do you HAVE to sing about food?

TONY: Well, how's this . . . *(sings)* "On the first day of Christmas, my true love gave to me a partridge in a pear tree. . . ."

BOB: I love pears.

LINDA: How 'bout *(sings)* "We wish you a merry Christmas . . ."

BOB *(thinks for a moment)*: I guess that sounds safe enough.

CAROLERS *(continue singing song)*: "We wish you a merry Christmas, We wish you a merry Christmas, and a happy new year. . . . Now, bring us some figgy pudding . . . Now, bring . . ."

BOB *(throws arms up in the air)*: Hold it! Hold it! *(To audience)* No wonder everyone gains weight during the holidays!

TONY: Hey, wait, I think someone's coming.

BOB: Of course. You've probably made them hungry!

(An elderly LADY opens the door.)

CAROLERS: MERRY CHRISTMAS!

LADY: Oh, my, what a surprise!

(CAROLERS *sing a short medley of Christmas carols.*)

LADY: That was lovely, just lovely! . . . I wish I had something to give you.

BOB: Have you had dinner yet?

TONY (*cutting him off*): Uh . . . look, there's no need to give us anything. We're just here to wish you a Merry Christmas and to share the love of Jesus with you.

LADY: You know, I was just wondering if I was going to have to spend another Christmas all alone. I'm so glad you came to my door.

LINDA: No one should have to spend Christmas alone. Look, our church is having a big Christmas dinner tomorrow night. Why don't you join us?

TONY: Yeah, there's going to be roast turkey, dressing, candied yams, cranberry sauce, mashed potatoes and gravy, tossed green salad, corn souffle, and plenty of pecan pie.

LADY: Oh, I'd just be in the way.

LINDA: In the way? Nonsense! You'll be our guest! So, what do you say?

LADY: You're sure you'll have enough for one more?

TONY: Positive. Now, we'll pick you up at seven o'clock, OK?

LADY: I'll be ready.

CAROLERS: Merry Christmas! (*They start to walk off.*)

LADY: Oh . . .

(CAROLERS *stop and turn around.*)

TONY: Yes?

LADY (*smiles*): Thanks.

(TONY *nods and smiles. She shuts the door.* CAROLERS *start toward the third door.*)

BOB (*to* TONY): Hey, you know, there's something I'd like to ask you.

TONY: What's that?

BOB: Why hasn't anyone mentioned this dinner to me before now?

TONY: We just wanted to make sure we had enough food for you.

BOB: Oh, I see. You were afraid you'd run out of turkey.

TONY: No, we were afraid Butterball would!

(Blackout.)

The Christmas Scramble

A Comedy Sketch

Characters:

TEACHER

CHILD NO. 1	CHILD NO. 8
CHILD NO. 2	CHILD NO. 9
CHILD NO. 3	CHILD NO. 10
CHILD NO. 4	CHILD NO. 11
CHILD NO. 5	CHILD NO. 12
CHILD NO. 6	CHILD NO. 13
CHILD NO. 7	CHILD NO. 14

Setting:

Stage should be decorated for annual Christmas program

Props:

Each child will need two signs. One will hang over neck in the front, and the other will hang over neck in the back. The signs should be prepared as follows:

	FRONT SIGN	REVERSE SIDE OF FRONT SIGN	BACK SIGN
CHILD NO. 1	T	M	H
CHILD NO. 2	M	E	A
CHILD NO. 3	S	R	P
CHILD NO. 4	I	R	P
CHILD NO. 5	A	Y	Y
CHILD NO. 6	M	C	(leave blank)
CHILD NO. 7	R	H	N
CHILD NO. 8	H	R	E
CHILD NO. 9	E	I	W
CHILD NO. 10	S	S	(leave blank)
CHILD NO. 11	R	T	Y
CHILD NO. 12	Y	M	E
CHILD NO. 13	R	A	A
CHILD NO. 14	C	S	R

Costumes:

Modern-day dress

▽

(Sketch opens with children taking their places on the stage. The cards hanging from their necks should spell out "TMSIAMRHESRYRC." The children begin their recitals . . .)

CHILD NO. 1: "T" is for the tinsel that we hang upon the tree.

CHILD NO. 2: "M" is for the many blessings that He gives to me.

CHILD NO. 3: "S" is for the snow that falls, so white and pure and clean.

CHILD NO. 4: "I" is for the icicles that decorate the scene.

CHILD NO. 5: "A" is for the angels who announced His holy birth.

CHILD NO. 6: "M" is for the manger that became His bed on earth.

CHILD NO. 7: "R" is for rejoicing as both heav'n and nature sing.

CHILD NO. 8: "H" is for the happiness that Baby Jesus brings.

CHILD NO. 9: "E" is for the eastern star that shined so clear and bright.

CHILD NO. 10: "S" is for the shepherds who watched o'er their flock by night.

CHILD NO. 11: "R" is for His royal birth, the Son of God is He.

CHILD NO. 12: "Y" is for the young Child who was born to set men free.

CHILD NO. 13: "R" is for remembering of what it is we sing.

CHILD NO. 14: "C" is for the Christ of Christmas, let His praises ring!

In Unison: And that spells . . . *(They look down at their cards)* . . . Tmsia Mrhesryrc?

(TEACHER comes on stage in a panic.)

TEACHER: My goodness! WHAT HAPPENED? Did you all grab the wrong letters?

CHILD NO. 3: Of course! We can't spell yet!

CHILD NO. 6: I KNEW something like this was going to happen!

CHILD NO. 9: Yeah. We should have just stuck to spelling "NOEL." It would have been so much easier.

CHILD NO. 1: Well, it's too late now.

CHILD NO. 10: Maybe the audience didn't notice.

CHILD NO. 8: I don't know. Something like this is pretty hard to ignore.

TEACHER: Well, we've still got to wish everyone a Merry Christmas, and how can we possibly do that when we're too busy wishing them a Tmsia Mrhesryrc?

CHILD NO. 4: Oh, is THAT what you're worried about?

CHILD NO. 13: THAT's no problem!

(The children quickly turn their front signs around revealing the correct "MERRY CHRISTMAS." Then they begin to sing . . .)

CHILDREN IN UNISON *(singing):*   We wish you a Merry Christmas,
We wish you a Merry Christmas,
We wish you a Merry Christmas,

TEACHER *(cuts in):* All right! All right! I'm impressed! But now, how are you going to wish them a Happy New Year?

(Children turn around, revealing their back signs, which spell out "HAPPY NEW YEAR." They look back over their shoulders, and finish song . . .)

CHILDREN IN UNISON *(singing):* And a Happy New Year!

Store Wars

A Comedy Sketch

Characters:
>MILLIE
>SARAH
>STORE CLERK

Setting:
>The Customer Complaint counter of a department store

Props:
>Sign saying "CUSTOMER COMPLAINT DEPARTMENT"
>A top or blouse
>A skirt
>Pen and paper
>"GONE SHOPPING" sign

Costumes:
>Modern-day dress

▽

(Sketch opens as MILLIE *[carrying top] and* SARAH *[carrying skirt] approach the customer complaint* CLERK, *each from opposite sides of the stage.)*

CLERK *(to* MILLIE): May I help you?

MILLIE: Is this the Customer Complaint Department?

CLERK: Yes, it is.

MILLIE: Good. I'd like to file a complaint.

CLERK: Very well. *(Takes out pen and paper.)* Now, then, tell me, ma'am, which product did not meet with your satisfaction?

MILLIE: Oh, I don't want to complain about a product. I want to complain about a customer.

CLERK: A customer? But we don't . . .

MILLIE: This IS the Customer Complaint Department, isn't it?

CLERK: Yes, but . . .

MILLIE: Well, I'm here to file a customer complaint. *(Looks at SARAH.)* . . . About HER!

SARAH: And I'm COUNTER-FILING!

MILLIE: Look, lady, YOU'RE the one who caused a scene.

SARAH: A scene?

MILLIE: Well, what would YOU call it when someone throws herself on the sale rack and cries, "I regret I have but one life to give for a bargain!"

SARAH: It's Christmas Eve. These are desperate times.

CLERK: Well, obviously, you were both able to find something you liked. *(To MILLIE)* You've got a nice blouse. *(To SARAH)* And you've got a nice skirt. So, what's the problem?

SARAH AND MILLIE *(in unison, holding up top and skirt):* This used to be a dress.

MILLIE: Yeah, till SHE wouldn't let go of it.

SARAH: I let go of it . . . when the police came.

CLERK: The police?

SARAH: Personally, I don't know why they were called in. The National Guard was doing fine.

CLERK: The National Guard? Uh, perhaps you'd better start at the beginning.

SARAH: Well, all right. You see, I was over in Housewares minding my own Christmas shopping business when all of a sudden the announcer came over the P.A. saying that all the dresses in Ladies' Wear were going on sale. Well, naturally, I started hyperventilating right there by the juicers. And just as soon as I composed myself, I walked calmly over to Ladies' Wear. . . .

MILLIE: She slid down the escalator.

SARAH: I CALMLY slid down the escalator. Then proceeded to Ladies' Wear.

MILLIE: She trampled 24 shoppers along the way.

SARAH: I said, "Excuse me."

MILLIE: Not to that one lady you knocked unconscious.

SARAH: She was a mannequin.

MILLIE: Yeah. Now.

CLERK: Look, ladies, it's Christmas Eve. This is a time for love, peace, and . . .

SARAH: Last-minute bargains.

CLERK: It's a time for giving . . .

MILLIE: So, then, why doesn't she give me back the bottom half of my dress?

CLERK: It's a time for showing goodwill toward men.

MILLIE: Hey, the men were fine. THEY got out of my way. SHE was the problem!

CLERK: Well, what do you say we show the spirit of the holiday, and just forget this entire little incident ever happened?

MILLIE: But . . .

CLERK *(smiles):* For the sake of Christmas.

SARAH: But what about the police report?

CLERK: I'll take care of that.

MILLIE: And the National Guard?

CLERK: They're used to Christmas sales.

SARAH: Well, what about the president?

CLERK: HE was called, too?

MILLIE *(nods):* Luckily, he just had his answering machine on.

CLERK: Well, don't worry. I'll leave another message explaining. So, what do you say? Truce?

SARAH *(thinks for a moment then extends her hand toward* MILLIE*):* Truce?

MILLIE *(smiles and extends her hand):* Truce. *(They shake.)*

ANNOUNCER *(over P.A.):* Attention, shoppers! There's a sale on shirts and slacks going on right now in our Men's Department. (SARAH *and* MILLIE *look at each other.*) I repeat, there is a sale in progress now in our Men's Department.

(SARAH *and* MILLIE *look at each other again, then take a slow, nonchalant step backward. They turn and look at each other once more, and take another slow step backward. Finally, they turn and look at each other again, then race offstage.*)

CLERK: Oh, well, you know what they say—if you can't beat 'em . . . *(hangs up "Gone Shopping" Sign.)* . . . you're just not running fast enough! (CLERK *darts offstage.*)

(Blackout.)

O Blessed Night of Stagefright

A Comedy Monologue

Character:

KEN

Setting:

Typical Christmas program set

▽

(We open with KEN *poking his head around stage curtain or doorway, which-ever applies. He takes a long, petrified look at the audience.)*

Do they honestly expect me to go out there in front of all those people and recite a Christmas poem? Are they crazy?! The place is packed!

And anyway, I don't remember volunteering for a part in the Christmas program. I was just scratching my head, and the teacher called on me. Me, of all people! I HATE talking in front of an audience. I can't even talk to myself without my knees shaking!

And look, there's Dad down in front with the video camera. It's not bad enough I'm going to mess up in front of the entire church. He has to get it on tape and show it to my grandchildren!

And there's Mom and Aunt Martha. They're motioning for me to get out there. In fact, isn't that a dollar bill Mom's waving? . . . Does she *really* think that's going to convince me to go out on stage? . . . Brad's mom gave him a five!

Uh-oh, now my teacher's motioning for me to get out there. Oh, well, the Bible says the Lord will go with us anywhere. So, I guess that includes centerstage. *(He walks over and stands centerstage. Taking a deep breath, he recites his poem. He's a little nervous at first, but ends up with an academy award winning performance)*

Rejoice, Rejoice, sing out in joy!
  A king is born this day!
Mary's little baby boy,
  Asleep upon the hay.

God's only Son has come to earth.
  Let all the world rejoice!
And celebrate His holy birth.
  Lift up, lift up your voice!

(Proudly to himself) Hey, that wasn't so bad after all. In fact, I could get used to being up here. This stagelife is pretty neat. Being in the spotlight, having the audience's undivided attention, getting my name in the program. And the Lord helped me not to forget any of my lines. *(Poses for the camera.)* Say, I hope Dad's getting my good side. *(Strikes another pose.)* And just think, he's still got five-and-a-half more hours of videotape left. Maybe I should say the poem again. Maybe I should lead the song service. Maybe I should take an offering.

No, on second thought, I'd better not. My teacher's signaling for me to cut, and now Mom's waving a tenspot just to get me off the stage.

All right, all right, I'm going, but now that I'm a seasoned performer *(throws his head back in sheer confidence)*, next year I'm holding out for a three-act!

'Tis Better to Give . . .

A Comedy Sketch

Characters:

CHARLES
PETER
PETER'S MOTHER

Setting:

A toy store window

Props:

A long, long roll of note paper, rolled tightly to look small
A pencil
Various toys on display in the store window, including:
 A remote control car
 Bow and arrow
 Box marked "MEN OF THE FUTURE ROBOT SET"
Another box marked "MEN OF THE FUTURE ROBOT SET," only this one's wrapped

Costumes:

Warm clothing
Peter and his mother are both dressed in old, worn clothes.
Charles is dressed in new and expensive clothes.

     ▽

(Sketch opens with CHARLES *looking in the store window and writing down his Christmas list on the note paper.* PETER *approaches.)*

PETER: Whatcha doing?

CHARLES *(continuing to write)*: Making out my Christmas list.

PETER: On that little piece of paper?

CHARLES *(unrolls note so audience can see it's about 10 feet long)*: I've been here awhile. So, what about you? Have you made out your list yet?

PETER: Naw. I don't go in for that sort of thing.

CHARLES: But then, how do your parents know what to buy you?

PETER *(starts to walk away)*: I really should be . . .

CHARLES *(cutting him off)*: Oh, wow! Look! *(He points at something in the window.)* A remote control car! Just what I've ALWAYS wanted! . . . And it's authentic! It comes with its own traffic jam! *(Writes it down on his list.)* Oh, I want that more than anything else in the world!

PETER: More than ANYTHING?

CHARLES: Well, except maybe for THAT! *(He points to the bow and arrow.)* Look! Over there in the corner. See that bow and arrow? It's just like Cochise's!

PETER *(impressed)*: Really? *(Presses against the window for a closer look.)* But, when was Cochise ever in Hong Kong?

CHARLES *(he writes it down anyway)*: Oh, if I got that, I wouldn't ask for anything else!

PETER: Nothing else?

CHARLES: Except maybe for THAT! *(Pointing)* Wow! Look! A genuine build-to-scale dinosaur construction set!

PETER: Is your house big enough for that?

CHARLES: Are you kidding? I've already got the tyrannosaurus rex in our dining room. 'Course we had to put in a sun roof to make room, but it fits. *(Starts writing.)* Now, let's see, I need the brontosaurus, the stegosaurus, the . . .

PETER: You really think your parents will buy you all those presents?

CHARLES: You should see all the presents under our Christmas tree already.

PETER: But they're not all for you, are they?

CHARLES: Only 33, but that figure's increasing at a rate of 10 percent . . . computed daily.

PETER: You compute the growth of your Christmas gifts?

CHARLES: Doesn't everybody? So, tell me, how many presents are you up to?

PETER *(bluffing)*: Oh, after the first 50, I kind of lost track.

CHARLES: You've got *50* presents under your tree?

PETER: Under the tree, down the hall, up the stairs, and into the library. Why, you can't even walk in my house without tripping over one of my gifts.

CHARLES: You're putting me on.

PETER: No, really, I've got . . .

(PETER'S MOTHER *enters and sees* PETER *in front of the toy store.*)

PETER'S MOTHER: So, there you are! I've been looking all over for you! But I should have known you'd be here at the toy store. Now, come on, quit your dreaming. I told you things are tight this Christmas. With your father ill and only my check coming in, we just can't afford to buy presents this year.

PETER (*to* CHARLES): I've got to go, I guess.

CHARLES: But, your mother said . . .

PETER (*cutting in*): See you around, OK?

CHARLES: But she said you weren't getting any presents.

PETER: It's no big deal. Really.

CHARLES: No big deal? Are you kidding? I'd rather do without a birthday party than not get any Christmas presents.

PETER: You would?

CHARLES: Well, no, but I couldn't think of another example.

PETER'S MOTHER: We'd better be going, Peter. It's getting late. (*They start to walk away, but* CHARLES *stops them.*)

CHARLES: Wait a minute! Don't go yet. I need to run home for something.

PETER: But . . .

CHARLES: Just stay right here. This won't take long. (*He darts offstage.*)

PETER'S MOTHER: What's he going home to get?

PETER: I don't know. Maybe he needs more paper.

PETER'S MOTHER: Huh?

PETER: Never mind.

PETER'S MOTHER (*looking in store window*): They sure decorate these windows pretty, don't they?

PETER: Yes, ma'am.

PETER'S MOTHER: So, which toy is it that's kept you here when you should have been home doing your chores?

PETER (pointing): That "Men of the Future Robot Set" there in the back. Isn't that the most terrific toy you ever saw in your life?

PETER'S MOTHER: Yeah, but look at that price tag. Is that for the toy or for the whole store?

(CHARLES rushes in, out of breath. He is carrying a beautifully wrapped package. He hands it to PETER.)

CHARLES: Here. This is for you.

PETER: For me? But I don't understand.

CHARLES: Take it. I want you to have it.

PETER (looks it over): But it says here, "To CHARLES."

CHARLES: So? Change your name. (Smiles.) No, really, I want you to have it. I've got enough presents.

PETER: But what about your computations?

PETER'S MOTHER: Computations?

PETER: He'll be a gift short now. He'll have to refigure everything.

CHARLES: No problem. I haven't made up the official inventory list yet, anyway.

PETER (pauses a moment): You're sure?

CHARLES: C'mon, open it. I insist.

(PETER rips open the package.)

PETER: Mother! Look! It's a Men of the Future Robot Set!

CHARLES (surprised): It is?

PETER: Oh, this is just what I wanted!

CHARLES (looking a bit sick, he mumbles under his breath): Me, too.

PETER'S MOTHER (to CHARLES): Are you sure you want to give this up?

CHARLES (still in shock): I thought it was socks.

PETER: What was that?

CHARLES: Uh, er, I said I thought you'd like it.

PETER: Like it? I LOVE it! This is the greatest toy in the world!

PETER'S MOTHER: But what about your parents?

CHARLES: They don't play with toys anymore. I had to make them stop. They were breaking too many.

PETER'S MOTHER: No, I mean will they mind you giving away one of your gifts like this?

CHARLES: I'll tell them, but they'll never believe me. You see, I've kind of got a reputation when it comes to presents.

PETER'S MOTHER: Well, anyway, that was a very generous thing to do.

CHARLES: You know what they say—it's better to give than to receive. Merry Christmas.

PETER: Merry Christmas to you, too! And THANKS!

PETER'S MOTHER (*to* PETER): Well, come on, Son. We've got to get home.

PETER (*as they're walking off*): Can you believe this, Mom? My very own Men of the Future Robot Set! (*They exit.*)

CHARLES (*looking over his Christmas list again*): Hmmm, now let's see. I'll just make that TWO Men of the Future Robot Sets. (*He marks it on his list.*) That way, he can have his set, and I'll still get another one. Oh, man, sometimes I truly amaze myself!

(PETER *reenters.*)

PETER: I just had to say thanks one more time. This is going to be my best Christmas ever!

CHARLES: I think it's going to be a pretty good one for me, too. (*They smile.* PETER *exits.*) Now, where was I? (*He looks down at list.*) Oh, yeah, that was TWO robot sets. (*Pauses for a moment.*) On second thought, maybe I don't need two. That one Men of the Future Robot Set has brought me enough joy already!

The Twelve Months of Christmas

A Comedy Sketch
(with music)

Characters:

Twelve SINGERS (one for each month)

Setting:

A Christmas theme set

Props:

JANUARY SINGER—a gift he (or she) is returning
FEBRUARY SINGER—a stack of bills (real ones will do)
MARCH SINGER—a dried-up tree with one ornament
APRIL SINGER—no props needed
MAY SINGER—a long string of Christmas lights wrapped around
        singer
JUNE SINGER—overnight bag
JULY SINGER—wallet, full of credit cards
AUGUST SINGER—broken appliance
SEPTEMBER SINGER—long scroll, blank
OCTOBER SINGER—bank statement and a penny
NOVEMBER SINGER—no props needed
DECEMBER SINGER—armful of wrapped packages

Costumes:

Modern-day dress
APRIL SINGER should be wearing the biggest, ugliest tie imaginable.

NOTE: If you make an appeal to your congregation, they'll probably gladly donate hundreds.

▽

(Sketch opens as JANUARY SINGER *enters with gift and sings to the tune of "The Twelve Days of Christmas")*

JANUARY SINGER: On the first of January
                   The big parades begin
                   Of folks taking Christmas gifts back.

(FEBRUARY SINGER *enters with a handful of bills and takes his place along-side* JANUARY SINGER.)

FEBRUARY SINGER: On February second
                   Deferred payments are due.
                   In debt again!

JANUARY SINGER: And folks taking Christmas gifts back.

(MARCH SINGER *enters with dried-up tree and takes his place alongside* FEBRUARY SINGER.)

MARCH SINGER: On the third day of March
                   The trash man finally takes
                   Your dried tree.

FEBRUARY SINGER: In debt again.

JANUARY SINGER: And folks taking Christmas gifts back.

(APRIL SINGER *enters wearing ugly tie. He lines up with the others.*)

APRIL SINGER: On the fourth day of April
                   You write off as a loss
                   Your Christmas ties.

MARCH SINGER: Your dried tree.

FEBRUARY SINGER: In debt again.

JANUARY SINGER: And folks taking Christmas gifts back.

(MAY SINGER *enters wrapped in Christmas lights, unlit, of course. He also lines up with others.*)

MAY SINGER: On the fifth day of May
                   Those Christmas lights come down
                   FIN-AL-LY!

APRIL SINGER: Your Christmas ties.

MARCH SINGER: Your dried tree.

FEBRUARY SINGER: In debt again.

JANUARY SINGER: And folks taking Christmas gifts back.

(JUNE SINGER *enters with overnight bag.*)

JUNE SINGER:	On the sixth day of June All your Christmas guests Just now are leaving.
MAY SINGER:	FIN-AL-LY!
APRIL SINGER:	Your Christmas ties.
MARCH SINGER:	Your dried tree.
FEBRUARY SINGER:	In debt again.
JANUARY SINGER:	And folks taking Christmas gifts back.

(JULY SINGER *enters with wallet full of credit cards.*)

JULY SINGER:	On the seventh day of July Pre-Christmas sales begin. MasterCard's a'callin'. *(Opens wallet and lets credit cards unravel.)*
JUNE SINGER:	Guests now are leaving.
MAY SINGER:	FIN-AL-LY!
APRIL SINGER:	Your Christmas ties.
MARCH SINGER:	Your dried tree.
FEBRUARY SINGER:	In debt again.
JANUARY SINGER:	And folks taking Christmas gifts back.

(AUGUST SINGER *enters with broken appliance.*)

AUGUST SINGER:	On the eighth day of August Your warranties expire. Gifts now are breaking.
JULY SINGER:	MasterCard's a'callin'.
JUNE SINGER:	Guests now are leaving.
MAY SINGER:	FIN-AL-LY!
APRIL SINGER:	Your Christmas ties.
MARCH SINGER:	Your dried tree.
FEBRUARY SINGER:	In debt again.
JANUARY SINGER:	And folks taking Christmas gifts back.

(SEPTEMBER SINGER *enters with long, blank scroll.*)

SEPTEMBER SINGER: On the ninth of September
                     You make your Christmas list.
                     (Unrolls scroll) Nobody's on it!

AUGUST SINGER: Gifts now are breaking.

JULY SINGER: MasterCard's a'callin'.

JUNE SINGER: Guests now are leaving.

MAY SINGER: FIN-AL-LY!

APRIL SINGER: Your Christmas ties.

MARCH SINGER: Your dried tree.

FEBRUARY SINGER: In debt again.

JANUARY SINGER: And folks taking Christmas gifts back.

(OCTOBER SINGER *enters with bank statement and a penny.*)

OCTOBER SINGER: On the tenth of October
                     Your Christmas club account
                     Just earned a penny! *(Show audience penny.)*

SEPTEMBER SINGER: Nobody's on it.

AUGUST SINGER: Gifts now are breaking.

JULY SINGER: MasterCard's a'callin'.

JUNE SINGER: Guests now are leaving.

MAY SINGER: FIN-AL-LY!

APRIL SINGER: Your Christmas ties.

MARCH SINGER: Your dried tree.

FEBRUARY SINGER: In debt again.

JANUARY SINGER: And folks taking Christmas gifts back.

(NOVEMBER SINGER *enters and lines up.*)

NOVEMBER SINGER: On the eleventh of November
                     You simply cannot find
                     Those gifts you were a'hiding. *(Shrugs shoulders.)*

OCTOBER SINGER: Just earned a penny.

SEPTEMBER SINGER: Nobody's on it.

AUGUST SINGER: Gifts now are breaking.

JULY SINGER: MasterCard's a'callin'.

JUNE SINGER: Guests now are leaving.

MAY SINGER: FIN-AL-LY!

APRIL SINGER: Your Christmas ties.

MARCH SINGER: Your dried tree.

FEBRUARY SINGER: In debt again.

JANUARY SINGER: And folks taking Christmas gifts back.

(DECEMBER SINGER *enters with armful of wrapped packages.*)

DECEMBER SINGER: On the twelfth of December
                      It all starts once again—
                      The pushing and the shoving.

NOVEMBER SINGER: Those gifts you were a'hiding.

OCTOBER SINGER: Just earned a penny.

SEPTEMBER SINGER: Nobody's on it.

AUGUST SINGER: Gifts now are breaking.

JULY SINGER: MasterCard's a'callin'.

JUNE SINGER: Guests now are leaving.

MAY SINGER: FIN-AL-LY!

APRIL SINGER: Your Christmas ties.

MARCH SINGER: Your dried tree.

FEBRUARY SINGER: In debt again.

JANUARY SINGER: And folks taking Christmas gifts back.

DECEMBER SINGER *(spoken):* You know, gang, Christmas doesn't have to be like this.

OTHER SINGERS *(spoken in unison):* It doesn't?

DECEMBER SINGER *(spoken):* Nope. Not if . . . *(Sings slowly, to the same tune)*

                      On the twenty-fifth of December
                      We'd bow our hearts to say . . .
                      Lord, Happy Birthday.

AUGUST SINGER *(spoken):* You know, he's right. Christmas means more than gifts that expire before their warranties.

FEBRUARY SINGER *(spoken):* And the two words you hear the most during the holidays should be "Merry Christmas," not "Charge it!"

NOVEMBER SINGER *(spoken):* Yeah, Christmas is far more special than that!

APRIL SINGER *(spoken):* Far more special, indeed!

(One by one the singers set their props down.)

ALL SINGERS *(in unison):* So . . . *(They sing)*
    On Christmas morning this year
    We'll bow our hearts to say . . .
    Lord, Happy Birthday!

Special Delivery

A Comedy Sketch

Characters:

> LETTER NO. 1
> LETTER NO. 2
> LETTER NO. 3

Setting:

A giant mailbox large enough for three performers to stand inside. The front of the mailbox facing the audience should be open so that the audience can see and hear the characters. There should be a mail slot above the characters' heads, and a pile of mail at the bottom of the mailbox.

Props:

Additional letters made out of poster board. Periodically throughout the sketch, someone from behind the mailbox (*out of the view of the audience*) will drop additional letters into the mail slot and on top of the letter characters. Also needed: A pen for LETTER NO. 1.

Costumes:

The three letter characters should tie a poster board around their necks. The poster boards can be made to look like letters by putting an address, return address, and a mock postage stamp on them.

▽

(Sketch opens with our letter characters standing inside the mailbox. LETTER NO. 1 is in the middle. LETTERS NOS. 2 and 3 are on either side of him. A pile of letters is being dumped on top of them.)

LETTER NO. 1 *(looks up to the top of the mailbox, then rubs his head)*: If they drop one more letter on my head, they're going to hear from me! *(Another letter is dropped directly on his head.)* That does it! I'm writing my Congressman! I'm writing the Postmaster General! I'm writing the president of the United States!

LETTER NO. 2: All right, but do me a favor. Wait till after the Christmas rush. It's crowded enough in here as it is!

LETTER NO. 3 *(looking upward):* And it's going to get even more crowded. Look! *(He points toward mail slot as another pile of letters is being dropped on them.)*

LETTER NO. 1: Hey, what do they think we are? Junk mail? I'm traveling first class. I don't have to put up with this! *(He gathers up some of the letters and starts to throw them back out through the slot.)*

LETTER NO. 3 *(stopping him):* Wait a minute! You can't just throw the guy's mail back at him.

LETTER NO. 1: You're right. I'll mark it "RETURN TO SENDER," then throw it at him! *(He starts writing on the letters and tossing them back out.)* And they say zip code moves the mail!

LETTER NO. 2 *(stopping him):* Look, it's the holiday stress that's getting to you. Try to calm down.

LETTER NO. 1: Calm down?! Are you kidding? Just look at me! I've got a torn return address, a wrinkled postage stamp, and quite frankly, I'm coming unglued!

LETTER NO. 3: You've been on the road awhile, eh?

LETTER NO. 1: I just returned from Europe.

LETTER NO. 2: EUROPE! And you're complaining?

LETTER NO. 1: I was only supposed to go across town.

LETTER NO. 3: Well, look at it this way, you got to see the world.

LETTER NO. 1: I hate to disillusion you, kid, but the inside of a mailbox isn't exactly Club Med. *(Looks up.)* Uh-oh, here we go again.

(Another pile of letters is dumped on them. LETTER NO. 1 *catches one on the way down and examines it.)*

LETTER NO. 1: Aha! Just as I thought. More Christmas cards.

LETTER NO. 2: You don't like Christmas cards?

LETTER NO. 1: Not from this angle. Besides, I never *could* figure out why people send Christmas cards at Christmas.

LETTER NO. 2: 'Cause they don't sell them in April.

LETTER NO. 3: Well, *I'm* a Christmas card.

LETTER NO. 2: You are?

LETTER NO. 3: Yes, and proud of it! I'm bringing a message of good cheer from one friend to another friend across the miles.

LETTER NO. 1: So then, why are you traveling postage due?

LETTER NO. 3: I guess they aren't *that* close of friends.

LETTER NO. 2: Well, I love Christmas cards. I find them warm and caring, and they always have something nice to say.

LETTER NO. 1 *(bends over and picks one up):* Yeah, like this one from Jake's Garage. The envelope says, "THIS CHRISTMAS, MAY GOOD CHEER ABIDE. MEANWHILE, YOU'LL FIND YOUR BILL INSIDE!"

LETTER NO. 2: Well, most Christmas cards send a little more sentiment than that.

LETTER NO. 3: All I know is when I arrive at my destination, I'm going to be greeted with a smile—after they pay the postage due, that is. And then, they'll probably put me on top of their mantel so everyone can see me. What do you think your people are going to do when they open you?

LETTER NO. 1: Cry. I'm from the I.R.S.

LETTER NO. 2 *(to* LETTER NO. 3*):* Well, I agree. Christmas cards do bring smiles to people.

LETTER NO. 3: And they let them know they're thought of.

LETTER NO. 1: I let people know they're thought of.

LETTER NO. 2: Somehow I don't think it's the same. *(Looks upward.)* Watch out! Another yuletide avalanche coming down. *(More letters are dropped.)*

LETTER NO. 3 *(excited):* Isn't this great! All these messages of peace and goodwill!

LETTER NO. 1 *(grumbling):* Yeah, and just think, there's only _____ *(fill in the number)* more days to go before CHRISTMAS! *(As more letters are dropped, he yells . . .)* HEEEEELLLLLPPPPPPP!

(Blackout.)

You're on the Air

A Comedy Sketch

Characters:

ANNOUNCER
Nine children:
BRENDA
MICHAEL
BILLY
RENEE
RUSTY
JOANN
ALVIN
BECKY
CASSIE

Setting:

Street corner

Props:

Microphone

Costumes:

Warm clothing

▽

(Sketch opens with the children looking in a store window. They are oohing and ahhing and pointing to the various things on display. Announcer steps on the scene.)

ANNOUNCER *(to audience):* Christmas means different things to different people. And so tonight our cameras are going to take you to the streets of _____ *(Insert town)* _____ to see just exactly what Christmas means to people there. *(Notices children on street corner)* Ah, I see some young children standing on the corner. Why don't we go over and ask what Christmas means to them. *(Walks over to the kids on stage.)* Hello. I'm with the "Camera on the Country" TV show. *(To* BRENDA) Have you watched our program?

BRENDA: No.

ANNOUNCER *(stunned):* You haven't? *(Trying to redeem himself, he continues . . .)* Well, I bet your mommy's watched us.

BRENDA: Oh, yes. She watches you all the time. She likes comedies.

ANNOUNCER *(chuckles):* No, no. This is the "Camera on the Country" TV show. We're not a comedy.

BRENDA: You're not? Then, how come she's always laughing?

ANNOUNCER *(to audience):* Out of all the corners in America, I had to pick this one. *(To* BRENDA) Well, anyway, the reason we're here tonight is to find out what Christmas means to you.

BRENDA: Oh, that's easy. Christmas means music. You know, Christmas carols. I LOVE Christmas carols.

ANNOUNCER: You do? Well, do you think you could sing one for us?

BRENDA: ARE YOU KIDDING?! You mean, right here? On national television? In front of millions and millions of people? Without any rehearsal or anything?! *(She grabs the microphone out of* ANNOUNCER'S *hand.)* You'd better believe it!

(Since this is her big chance for stardom, she takes over the stage, and proceeds to "belt out" a selected traditional Christmas carol. Preferably, it should be upbeat. After her number, she rejoins the CHILDREN.)

ANNOUNCER *(tries to get the microphone back from her. They wrestle for a moment. He finally wins, then looks toward audience . . .):* Shy little girl, isn't she? *(Turns to* MICHAEL.) And now, let's find out what Christmas means to this young man. Hello, sir. You look intelligent. I bet you've watched our show.

MICHAEL: No. That's why I still look intelligent.

BILLY *(to* ANNOUNCER): Hey, I know you!

ANNOUNCER *(flattered):* You do? *(To* BILLY) I don't mean to cross in front of you, but . . . *(Stands directly in front of* BILLY.)

MICHAEL: Yeah, you're from "Camera on the Country," aren't you?

ANNOUNCER: That's right. I guess you've seen me on TV, huh?

MICHAEL: Just as a blur. You know, as I'm turning the channel to the good programs.

ANNOUNCER (*steps back, and says to* BILLY): So, as I was saying . . .

BILLY: You want to know what Christmas means to me?

ANNOUNCER: Yes, that's right.

BILLY: Christmas means presents.

ANNOUNCER: And which do you like better—giving or receiving?

BILLY: Both. I like giving hints and receiving what I asked for.

ANNOUNCER: And what did you ask for this year?

BILLY: Mattel.

ANNOUNCER: OK, Mattel makes it. But what's the name of the toy?

BILLY: No, you don't understand. I want MATTEL. I want controlling stock in the company.

ANNOUNCER (*looks toward audience*): Whatever happened to only wanting their two front teeth?

BILLY: Don't need them. I've got caps.

ANNOUNCER (*to* RENEE): And what about you? What does Christmas mean to you?

RENEE: It means shopping. Crowded stores. Christmas specials. People pushing and shoving. Why, do you know I got lost the other night in the new shopping mall?

ANNOUNCER: Well, you really should have been holding onto your mother's hand.

RENEE: I was! She was the one who got us lost!

RUSTY: I say Christmas means food!

ANNOUNCER: Food?

RUSTY: Yeah, lots of food. Turkey, dressing, cranberry sauce, rolls, butter, mashed potatoes and gravy . . .

ANNOUNCER (*to* JOANN): And what does Christmas mean to you?

RUSTY: Hey! I wasn't finished. That was just the appetizers!

JOANN: I say Christmas means decorating the Christmas tree.

ALVIN: I say Christmas cards.

BECKY: Well, what about Christmas lights?

ANNOUNCER: This is great! Those are all terrific answers!

CASSIE: Excuse me.

ANNOUNCER: Yes?

CASSIE: You're right. Those are terrific answers. But Christmas means something far more important than all of that.

BILLY: More important than presents?

BRENDA: More important than my heartwarming rendition of *(insert title of song)*.

RUSTY: More important than leftover turkey sandwiches?

ANNOUNCER: Certainly not more important than "Camera on the Country."

CASSIE: Christmas is Jesus' birthday. And while the gifts, the carols, the dinners, and even "Camera on the Country" are all good . . .

ANNOUNCER: . . . Would you like to be my cohost?

CASSIE *(continuing)*: We should never forget whose day it really is.

ANNOUNCER: In other words, when we celebrate His birthday, let's be sure we include Him.

CASSIE: Yeah, that's it exactly. That way, Christmas will always mean something special to all of us.

(Blackout.)

Oh, Christmas Tree! Oh, Christmas Tree!

A Comedy Sketch

Characters:

> RUSS
> MARSHA

Setting:

> Russ and Marsha's living room

Props:

> 2 Christmas trees with more bald spots than Telly Savalas
> Tinsel garland
> Ornaments
> Christmas tree lights
> Treetop

▽

(Sketch opens with MARSHA *sitting on the sofa.* RUSS *opens the front door, and just sticks his head in.)*

RUSS: Are you ready?

MARSHA *(excited):* I'm ready.

RUSS: Really ready?

MARSHA: Really ready.

RUSS: Really, really ready?

MARSHA *(to audience):* Boy, he sure knows how to stretch out his part, doesn't he?

RUSS *(comes on in, bringing a tree with him):* Surrrrrprise!

MARSHA (unimpressed): What's THAT?

RUSS: Our Christmas tree! (He sets it up.) So, what do you think?

MARSHA (looking it over): The neighbors didn't see you bring it in, did they?

RUSS (proudly): I got it on sale. Half off.

MARSHA: Tell me, did that half off refer to the price or to the branches?

RUSS: All right, I admit it is a little bare.

MARSHA: A little bare? Are you kidding? The wind didn't just whistle through those branches. It sang operas!

RUSS: All it needs is some fixing up. You know, some tinsel garland.

MARSHA: Yeah, so it won't catch cold!

RUSS: And some ornaments.

MARSHA: Keeping them even on each side so it won't fall over.

RUSS: And a nice treetop ornament.

MARSHA: For a lightning rod, no doubt!

RUSS: Something tells me you don't like this tree.

MARSHA: Oh, I'm sure it was pretty at the store, but dragging it home behind the car didn't do it much good.

RUSS: Actually, this is exactly how it looked at the store.

MARSHA: Oh, I get it. It was the only one left.

RUSS: No, they had plenty of nice, beautiful, full ones. But this one sort of caught my attention.

MARSHA: The termites were making too much racket, huh?

RUSS: Go ahead and laugh. But you'll see. This is going to be the prettiest tree we've ever had. Now then, we'll just hang up a few bulbs. (He hangs some ornaments on the tree.)

MARSHA: It's already starting to lean.

RUSS: And we'll string some lights. (He wraps a strand of lights around tree.)

MARSHA: I hope they're the flashing kind, so half the time it'll be in the dark.

RUSS: And some tinsel . . . *(He hangs up tinsel.)*

MARSHA: Are you sure this tree is strong enough to hold all that?

RUSS *(continuing with the decorating):* . . . And some more ornaments.

MARSHA: You're pushing your luck.

RUSS: And finally, a nice treetop. *(He places the treetop on top of the tree, then stands back to admire it.)* Now, tell me the truth, is this or is this not the most beautiful tree you ever laid your eyes on?

MARSHA *(still unimpressed):* That is, without a doubt, the most . . . *(RUSS turns on the lights. They both stop and look at it. It does look rather beautiful.)* That is one of the loveliest trees we've ever had.

RUSS: That's because the real beauty of a Christmas tree isn't how full it is, or how tall it is, or even how elaborately it's decorated. The real beauty is in what it stands for . . . and that's Christ's birthday.

MARSHA: You know, you're right. It doesn't matter if you've got a 30-foot tree or just a twig with a bow on it. The important thing is to remember what we're celebrating.

RUSS: So, you're happy with it?

MARSHA: Of course, I am, dear.

RUSS: Good, 'cause it wasn't actually half off.

MARSHA: Don't tell you paid FULL PRICE for this tree!

RUSS: No. *(He goes out the door, and brings in another equally puny tree.)* It was a two-for-one sale!

The Recitation

A Comedy Sketch

Characters:

> Dave
> Anita
> Mother

Setting:

> The characters' living room

Props:

> Script

Costumes:

> Modern-day dress
> Angel costume for Anita *(for later in the sketch)*
> Shepherd costume for Dave *(for later in the sketch)*

▽

(Sketch opens with Dave *sitting on the sofa reading a magazine.* Anita, *his younger sister, is studying for her part in the Christmas program. She has her script in hand.)*

Anita *(dramatically):*   Christmas comes but once a year,
And so let's fill our hearts with cheer,
And tell all those that we hold dear . . .

Dave: How long are we going to have to listen to this?

Anita: Until I have it memorized.

Dave: Doesn't it count if me and all the neighbors have it memorized?

Anita *(igoring him):*   Christmas comes but once a year,
And so let's fill our hearts with cheer,
And . . .

DAVE *(cutting in):* stuff some cotton in our ear!

ANITA *(calling offstage):* Mommy!

DAVE: Oh, all right, all right. I'll leave you alone.

ANITA *(continuing):*   Christmas comes but once a year,
And so let's fill our hearts with cheer,
And tell all those that we hold dear . . .

DAVE *(cutting in):* . . . Thank God the Christmas pageant's near!

ANITA *(whining):* You promised!

DAVE: OK, but I still say you're going about this all wrong.

ANITA: How's that?

DAVE: You're in the same room I am. Why don't you find some place more private . . . like Iceland.

ANITA: I take it you've already got YOUR part memorized.

DAVE: No, but it'll only take me a few minutes.

ANITA: To memorize it?

DAVE: No, to write it down on my palm.

ANITA: You're going to write your entire recitation on the palm of your hand?

DAVE: Not the ENTIRE recitation, silly. Only part of it. The rest will have to go up my arms.

ANITA: But that's crazy! How are you going to read your arms during the Christmas program?

DAVE: I'll just have to make sure I'm always in the spotlight.

ANITA: Well, I still say it's better to memorize it. A Christmas poem is more than just something you say one time then forget about it. It should be something that stays with you forever.

DAVE: Oh, you mean like your pancakes?

ANITA *(offended):* You said you liked my pancakes.

DAVE: I do. I'm using them to keep my bed level.

ANITA *(folds arms and sings):* Sticks and stones may break my bones . . .

DAVE *(continuing song):* . . . But you'll still put them in the batter!

ANITA: There's no talking to you. So, go ahead, use your cheat notes.

DAVE *(looks at palm of his hand):* I prefer to call them Hand Hints.

ANITA: Hand Hints, Elbow Essays . . . whatever you want to call them, it's still taking the easy way out. And years from now you won't even remember what you got up on stage and said.

DAVE: Oh, I don't know. Maybe I'll never wash.

ANITA: Well, *I'M* going to memorize *MY* part. I'm going to ALWAYS remember it, and LEARN from it. *(Starts practicing again.)*
. . . Christmas comes but once a year,
And so let's fill our hearts with cheer,
And tell all those that we hold dear . . .

(MOTHER enters, carrying their costumes.)

MOTHER: Your teacher just brought over your costumes for the pageant. Here's yours, Anita. *(She hands her the angel costume.)* And here's yours, Dave. *(She hands him the shepherd's costume.)* Try them on. See if they fit.

(DAVE and ANITA quickly slip the costumes over their clothes.)

DAVE *(disappointed):* Hey, wait a minute! This has long sleeves!

MOTHER: You were hoping to get a tan from the spotlight?

DAVE: It didn't say anything in the script about LONG sleeves.

ANITA: They didn't really have tank tops in those days, Dave.

MOTHER: Long sleeves, short sleeves, it doesn't really matter, does it?

ANITA: Not if the script calls for a shepherd with laryngitis.

MOTHER: Huh?

DAVE: Uh, nothing, Mom. The costume's fine.

MOTHER: Good. Now, go back to memorizing your parts.

(MOTHER exits.)

ANITA: Well, now what are you going to do?

DAVE *(thinks for a moment):* You're sure they didn't have tank tops back then?

ANITA: I think it's on record.

DAVE: How 'bout a T-shirt that says "SHEPHERDS ARE LEADERS IN THEIR FIELD"?

ANITA: Doubt it.

DAVE: Well, then, I guess there's only one thing left to do.

ANITA: What's that?

DAVE *(grabs her script and starts practicing his part):*
> . . . While the shepherds watched their flocks at night
> They looked and saw a wondrous sight . . .

(While DAVE *finishes his recitation piece,* ANITA *continues practicing hers at the same time.)*

DAVE	ANITA
A host of angels shone so bright	And tell all those that we hold dear
And told the miracle.	That Jesus Christ is born.
While shepherds watched their flocks by night,	Christmas comes but once a year,
They looked and saw a wondrous sight . . .	And so let's fill our hearts with cheer . . .

(They continue practicing to blackout.)

(Blackout.)

The Relative

A Comedy Sketch

Characters:

> Norma
> Bob
> Uncle Milfred

Setting:

> Typical living room set: sofa, easy chair, television, etc. Set should have a front door, a bedroom door, and a front room window; however, if need be, these may be mimed.

Props:

> 4 or 5 pieces of bulging luggage

Sound Effects:

> Doorbell

Costumes:

> Modern-day dress

▽

(Sketch opens with Bob *asleep in easy chair. The television set is on, and* Bob *is snoring. The doorbell rings.)*

Bob *(waking up):* Wouldn't you know it? Right in the middle of my program! *(He begrudgingly walks over and turns off the set. He proceeds to the front door and opens it. We clearly see it's* Uncle Milfred *and his overstuffed luggage.)* If you're selling it, I don't want it. If you're looking for it, I ain't got it, and if you're . . .

Uncle Milfred *(cutting in):* Merry Christmas!

Bob: Merry Christmas to you, too, but if that's luggage you're selling, we don't need any. *(He shuts the door, then starts walking back to the sofa.*

The doorbell rings again. He walks back and opens the door.) Look, Buddy, didn't you hear me?

UNCLE MILFRED: No, no, I'm afraid you don't understand. This is MY luggage. I believe we're related.

BOB *(brief pause while he looks down at luggage):* Sorry, but I make it a point not to know anyone who owns that much luggage.

UNCLE MILFRED: Pardon me?

BOB *(laughs, realizing the man is serious):* Just kidding. Now, don't tell me, let me guess. Uh . . . Uh . . .

UNCLE MILFRED: Uncle Milfred.

BOB: Oh, well, of course. Uncle Milfred. Why, I haven't seen you in . . . Well, tell me, just how long has it been, Uncle Milfred?

UNCLE MILFRED: You've never seen me. I'm your wife's uncle.

BOB: Oh, THAT Uncle Milfred. Yes. Yes. I've heard her speak of you many times. Come in! Come in! I'll go get her now. *(He walks over to bedroom door and calls out to her.)* Uh, dear . . .

(Meanwhile, UNCLE MILFRED *begins bringing in his luggage. When* NORMA *enters, his back is to her, and he doesn't notice.)*

BOB *(under his breath to* NORMA*):* How come you've never mentioned you had an Uncle Milfred?

NORMA: An uncle who?

BOB: Milfred. You know, spindly legs, hairy arms, scraggly beard.

NORMA: That sounds like my Aunt Alice.

BOB: He said his name is Milfred, and he's your uncle.

NORMA *(pointing):* That's him, huh?

BOB: It ain't the Avon lady.

NORMA: Well, I sure don't remember him.

BOB: Don't worry. From the looks of his luggage, you're going to have plenty of time to get reacquainted! In fact, I'm surprised he didn't bring a U-Haul!

UNCLE MILFRED *(bringing in the last piece of luggage):* Well, I guess that'll do it for now. The rest of my things are out in the U-Haul.

BOB *(to himself):* There are no surprises left in this world.

UNCLE MILFRED (*looks up and sees* NORMA): My goodness, would you look at you! You're all grown up!

BOB: I'm the same size I was a minute ago. . . . Oh, you meant her.

NORMA: Uncle Milfred! It's so good to see you again! (*They hug, but behind his back she shrugs to* BOB, *indicating she still doesn't remember him.*)

UNCLE MILFRED: I hope I'm not imposing.

NORMA: Are you kidding? We're thrilled to have you. Aren't we, dear?

BOB: Thrilled? (NORMA *kicks him.*) Yes, of course (*holding his leg*), I'm so happy, it hurts! So, tell me, Uncle Milfred, just how long can you stay with us?

NORMA: Honey, you shouldn't ask a question like that.

BOB: Well, it's just that I'm so excited, I'd like to know how much time Uncle Milfred's going to have to visit with us. A week? Or two? Or till Halley's Comet comes back?

UNCLE MILFRED: Why? Do you get a good view of it from here? . . . No, really, I appreciate your hospitality, but I don't think I can stay much past New Year's Day.

BOB: You do mean of THIS coming year, don't you?

NORMA (*kicking* BOB *again*): Uh, sweetheart, why don't you help Uncle Milfred bring in the rest of his things.

(BOB *limps over to window to look out.*)

UNCLE MILFRED: Oh, that's all right. We can get it later.

BOB (*looking out window*): My, my! You've got quite a load on that trailer. You must have had a time trying to fit through tunnels.

UNCLE MILFRED: You should have seen it before the piano fell off.

BOB: You packed a piano?

UNCLE MILFRED: Hey, it's not my fault they don't have entertainment at rest stops.

NORMA: Well, come on, Uncle Milfred. (*She sits on sofa.*) Sit down here and tell me how you've been and what you've been doing.

UNCLE MILFRED (*sitting on sofa next to her*): Well, to be perfectly honest, I've been awful lonely lately.

(BOB *sits in easy chair.*)

NORMA: Lonely?

UNCLE MILFRED *(teary-eyed)*: Yes, ever since . . . well, ever since your aunt went . . . you know, went on home, it's just been me and the ol' Ford out there. *(Pensive)* Funny, I always thought I'd be the one to go first, but I guess it just wasn't meant to be that way.

NORMA: I'm so sorry. When did she die?

UNCLE MILFRED: Die? She didn't die. She just went on home. Couldn't take all this traveling. But she did say to tell you "Hi."

NORMA: I would have liked seeing her again.

UNCLE MILFRED: Well, she's an awful lot like your mother, you know. And a lot like you. Opening your home to someone you haven't seen in ages. That's something they'd both do.

NORMA: But you're my uncle. You're family.

BOB: Besides, you heard the television. You knew we were home. (NORMA *kicks* BOB *again.*)

UNCLE MILFRED: What's that?

BOB *(holding his leg)*: I said, besides, you can't spend Christmas alone.

UNCLE MILFRED: Well, that's mighty generous of you, but you know, something tells me you'd do this even if I were a perfect stranger. You see, you two have the Christmas spirit. You don't see it much anymore, but you two sure have it.

BOB: The Christmas spirit?

UNCLE MILFRED: Sure, you know, showing kindness to your fellowman, spreading a little peace and goodwill, putting out the ol' holiday welcome mat.

BOB *(rising)*: Well, yes, I guess that is true. Our welcome mat is ALWAYS out. *(Walks over and opens door.)* See, there it is right there. It says, "TRESPASSERS WILL BE SHOT ON SIGHT!" *(Embarrassed)* Uh, dear? What happened to our *other* welcome mat?

NORMA: What one was that, sweetheart?

BOB: The one that said, "PEACE TO ALL WHO ENTER."

NORMA: Oh, yes. Wasn't that the one you threw at the last door-to-door salesman?

BOB (*to* UNCLE MILFRED): What can I say? I'm a giving person.

NORMA: Yeah, well, lucky for you she was a Girl Scout and knew how to duck.

UNCLE MILFRED: Well, anyway, I sure appreciate the kindness you've shown toward me. You don't know how refreshing it is to see someone keeping the spirit of Christmas alive. Especially nowadays.

BOB: Well, I, uh . . .

UNCLE MILFRED: No, it's true. People just don't care about people anymore. But you two do. Your warmth and your hospitality overwhelm me. You're quite a couple!

NORMA: Well, now, don't . . .

UNCLE MILFRED: No, I mean it. You've really made an old man feel special. Your mother, Rachel, must be very proud of you.

NORMA: My mother's name isn't Rachel.

UNCLE MILFRED: It isn't?

NORMA: No, it's Sarah.

UNCLE MILFRED: But isn't this 14 Bundy Lane?

NORMA: No, it's 28 Bundy Lane.

UNCLE MILFRED: Well, how do you like that! I'm in the wrong house. I'm so sorry.

BOB (*under his breath*): I'm so relieved.

UNCLE MILFRED: What's that?

BOB: Uh, I said, "Can you *believe* a mix-up like this?"

UNCLE MILFRED: Well, look, I'll just take my things and be on my way.

BOB (*handing him his suitcases*): What's your hurry?

UNCLE MILFRED: My niece is expecting me. They'll be worried. But listen, you know everything I said about you having the Christmas spirit and all? It still goes. (*He puts the suitcases down and takes their hands.*) You two have something special. Don't lose it. (*He turns and starts to pick up the suitcases again.*)

BOB (*changing his attitude*): Uh, . . . Uncle, I mean, . . . Milfred?

UNCLE MILFRED: Yes?

BOB: Listen, uh ... if your niece isn't home when you get there, why don't you come back here and stay with us? *(He looks over at* NORMA.*)* Did I just say that? (NORMA *nods).*

UNCLE MILFRED: Well now, I just might do that.

NORMA: We'd love to have you!

BOB: Yeah, after all, what's Christmas if you don't share it with someone? *(Looks over at* NORMA *again.)* Did I just say that, too? (NORMA *nods and smiles, obviously pleased with the change.)*

NORMA: In fact, Milfred, why don't you just make it a point to stop by here on a regular basis? You're kind of nice to have around!

UNCLE MILFRED: It'd be my pleasure. But next time *(he gathers up the suitcases)* I'll make sure I pack enough! *(He exits.)*

(Blackout.)

The Annual Gift Exchange

A Comedy Monologue

Character:

ANNE

Setting:

The annual church Christmas party

Costume:

Modern-day dress

▽

(Sketch opens with ANNE *standing center stage. She looks out toward the audience as if watching the gift table.)*

C'mon. When is it going to be MY turn for the gift exchange? All the BIG gifts are going like mints at a garlic festival! By the time I get up there, all that'll be left will be the dinky, little cheap ones—you know, like the one I brought.

I don't know why they do these gift exchanges anyway. If someone wants a $3.00 gift from me that bad, let her get on my Christmas list like everyone else.

Ummm. They just called Darlene. I can guess which gift she's going to pick. . . . Yep! I knew it! She's heading right for that big red package. Wouldn't you know it! The biggest, flashiest package on the table, and she's already got the ribbon ripped off! Doesn't she have any shame? Doesn't she know how greedy that looks? Doesn't she care what people think about her? DOESN'T SHE KNOW *I* WANTED THAT GIFT?!

Oh, well, at least the big green one's still left. . . . And it's Jennifer's turn. Jennifer HATES green. She'll, no doubt, take the little blue one over in the corner. Or perhaps that small yellow one there in the back. Or . . .

Hey, wait a minute! I thought Jennifer hated green! Well, you know what this means, don't you? If I'm going to get anything decent, I'll just have to trip someone on their way back to their seat. I hate to do it, but it worked last year!

No, wait. The silver one hasn't been taken yet. It's not as big as either the green one or the red one, but it IS wrapped in foil. And no one puts a cheap gift in expensive wrapping. . . . OK, sure, I did, but that was just to throw them off. For the past three years I've had to take my own gift back home with me. But this year I'm determined to get rid of it. I've put it in a bigger box, wrapped it in eye-catching purple foil, and even attached a matching bow. Somebody's GOT to take it!

No! No! Paula, wait! Not the SILVER one! Take the PURPLE one instead! It's the one *I* brought. . . . Well, there's no need to get personal. And anyway, what makes you think it's the car-jack keychain again? . . . Well, three years in a row is hardly predictable behavior. . . . No, no, go ahead. If you want the silver package, by all means, go for it. But, just don't call *me* the next time you get a flat!

So, now we're down to the last three gifts. . . . No, make that the last two. Marci just took the yellow one. . . . And look, now Teri's heading right for the blue one.

Boy! Wouldn't you know it! It's finally my turn, and the only gift left is the one I brought! And what am I going to do with a car-jack keychain? I've still got the electric melonballer and the pocket food processor I got at a gift exchange five years ago. And that's not even counting the blinking Christmas tie my husband got last year. It wouldn't have been so bad, but it was a plug-in!

But, wait! I still have the office Christmas party! *(Scheming.)* Maybe if I put my car-jack keychain in an even bigger box, wrap it in *gold* foil this time, put a HUGE bow on it, and . . .

(Looks upward, proudly.) Oh, yes, yes! When it comes to Christmas gift exchanges, sometimes it truly IS far better to give than to receive!

Mistletoe Macho

A Comedy Sketch

Cast:

PAUL
CHARLENE
MARY
SANDY

Setting:

An empty room or hall

Props:

A sprig of mistletoe and a string on which to hang it

Costumes:

Modern-day dress

▽

(Sketch opens with PAUL *entering and hanging up the mistletoe.)*

PAUL: Ah, there we go. It's all set. I'll just stand right here under this mistletoe and wait for the first lucky young lady to come along and be rewarded for her excellent good fortune and timing. Yessir, this is it, girls. This is your big day! But remember, no pushing and no taking cuts. *(Pauses for a moment, listening)* Ah-ha, I think I hear the crowd rushing in now. *(Listens for another moment.)* Yes, yes, I hear it. The crowd is rushing in now. *(Listens again, a little more impatiently.)* Right now, the crowd is rushing in. *(Finally,* CHARLENE *enters. He explains to the audience . . .)* The others must have gotten caught at the light. *(To* CHARLENE*)* Hello, Charlene. Notice anything special about where I'm standing?

CHARLENE: Yeah, you're in my way.

PAUL: No, silly, the mistletoe. I'm standing under mistletoe.

CHARLENE (looking up at mistletoe): Ah, yes, so you are. Doesn't give much shade, does it? See ya. (She walks offstage.)

PAUL (looks up at mistletoe; he's in shock): Maybe it's defective. Yeah, that's it. I'll write a letter and complain. The mistletoe quality control people are falling down on their job. . . . But, wait! I think I hear the thundering footsteps of the masses even as I speak. (He listens for a moment.) Yes, that's it. The thundering footsteps of the masses . . . even as I speak. (MARY enters. PAUL looks around for more, but is again disappointed. He explains to the audience . . .) Obviously, very noisy shoes.

MARY: I beg your pardon?

PAUL: Uhh . . . never mind. So, tell me, Mary, do you notice anything remarkable about where I'm standing?

MARY: Yeah. You're not in front of a mirror. (She exits.)

PAUL: I can't believe this! I'm being abandoned under the most romantic plant in the world. I mean, this isn't just anyone standing here. This is Paul the Doll! Where's my usual stampede?

(SANDY, a nice-looking but plain girl, enters.)

SANDY: Hi.

PAUL (uninterested): Oh, hi, Sandy.

SANDY (looking up at mistletoe): Isn't that mistletoe you're standing under?

PAUL: Yeah, but I think I'm getting my money back.

SANDY: Why? Doesn't it work?

PAUL: Let's just say I've seen bigger crowds at volunteer tax audits.

SANDY: Maybe you're trying too hard. Maybe you should just be yourself.

PAUL: Hey, I'm the same terrifically handsome guy I've always been.

SANDY: No, I mean your *real* self. Who you are down deep inside.

PAUL: Oh, nobody cares about that.

SANDY: God does.

PAUL: What do you mean?

SANDY: He knows the REAL Paul. The Paul who sometimes feels lonely.

PAUL: I didn't feel lonely till I stepped under this mistletoe!

SANDY: . . . And the Paul who pretends to have it all under control . . . even when he feels a little lost and frightened himself. He knows him, too.

PAUL *(more serious):* I didn't think anyone knew that Paul.

SANDY: God does, and He cares about him very much.

PAUL: So, what you're saying is God loves me—mistletoe or not.

SANDY: Something like that. But just to prove it's not defective . . . *(She kisses him on the cheek.)*

PAUL: Say, that stuff works pretty good after all! *(He thinks for a moment.)* Ummm, maybe I should freeze-dry some of it for the rest of the year. Or better yet, I'll have a suit made out of it. Or maybe even . . .

SANDY *(yanking him offstage):* A sure case of mistletoe overexposure if I've ever seen one.

I'll Be Home for Christmas . . . if I Ever Get Waited on at the Mall

---

A Comedy Sketch

Characters:

> LEROY
> FRANK
> 8 or 9 EXTRAS, male or female
> LADY SHOPPER

Setting:

> A department store. Leroy and extras should be lined up in a line that appears to continue offstage indefinitely.

Props:

> Each cast member should be carrying an item or items to be purchased.

Costumes:

> Modern-day dress

▽

(Sketch opens with LEROY *standing at the end of the line.* FRANK *enters and approaches* LEROY.)

FRANK: Excuse me, but is this the end of the line?

LEROY: It is unless you can get everyone to do an about-face.

FRANK: Well, it's just that I didn't expect the end of the line to be on a different floor from the register.

LEROY: Oh, this is nothing. You should see this place when they're crowded.

FRANK: I take it by the tone in your voice you don't enjoy Christmas shopping.

LEROY: Oh, I just get tired of all the pushing, shoving, and downright rudeness.

FRANK (*looking around*): Well, there doesn't seem to be much of that going on right now.

LEROY: Of course not. They made me stop.

FRANK (*brief pause*): So, what's that you're buying?

LEROY: Oh, this? I don't know what it's called, but it's EXACTLY what I was looking for.

FRANK: What does it do?

LEROY: Who knows, but it's *perfect.*

FRANK: But if you don't know what it is, and you don't know what it does, why are you buying it?

LEROY: Revenge. The person I'm giving it to always gives me worthless junk like this.

FRANK: Tell me, do you put this much love into all your gifts?

LEROY: Hey, if I didn't love the person, I wouldn't have gone to this much trouble to get even.

FRANK (*brief pause*): Boy, I still can't get over how long this line is.

LEROY: Yeah, all we'd have to do is turn sideways and hold hands, and we could make a fund-raiser out of it!

FRANK: Has it been moving very fast?

LEROY: Let me put it this way, see that lady up there pushing the stroller?

FRANK: Yeah?

LEROY: Well, when she first got in line, she was riding in it.

FRANK: I guess everyone waited till the last minute to go Christmas shopping, huh?

LEROY: All I know is I had to drive around this mall six times looking for a parking space. . . . I would have gone a seventh, but I was afraid the walls of J. C. Penney would come a'tumbling down.

FRANK: So where'd you finally park?

LEROY: In my driveway. I drove home and walked back.

FRANK: Well, at least you got your exercise for the day.

LEROY: Are you kidding? I've been walking since Monday. I live out of state.

(The first EXTRA *exits the stage giving the illusion the line is moving.)*

FRANK: Oh, good. The line's starting to move. *(They all move forward one space.)* So, is this it? Are you done with all your shopping now?

LEROY: MasterCard says I am.

FRANK: Reached your limit, eh?

LEROY *(nods):* I said, "MasterCard, take me away," and they said, "One more purchase and we will!"

FRANK: I know what you mean. I've used my cards so much this season, the numbers are bald. So, tell me, why do we do it?

LEROY: 'Cause there's no payment till February.

FRANK: No, I mean why do we go through all this hustle-bustle, the crowded stores, the fights over bargains. It didn't used to be this way, you know. I can remember when shoppers used to deck the halls . . . instead of each other.

LEROY: Times have changed.

FRANK: Yeah, nowadays even carolers have to carry mace.

LEROY: Christmas carolers . . . now there's an endangered species! The last guy to come to my door singing "Let It Snow" was the gas man shutting off my heat for nonpayment.

FRANK: What's happened to our Christmas spirit lately?

LEROY: I dunno. I guess chestnuts tend to lose something roasting in a microwave.

FRANK: Well, I say it's not too late to get it back. I say we can recapture that spirit of Christmas.

LEROY: How?

FRANK: By remembering what this day really means. Christmas is more than long lines at checkout counters, and bumper battles over premium parking spaces. It's a birthday celebration too special to be rushed . . . for a king too special to be forgotten.

LEROY *(thoughtfully):* I suppose sometimes we get so busy with Christmas, we forget to keep Christ in it.

FRANK: Sad, but too often very true.

(LADY SHOPPER *enters and approaches* FRANK *and* LEROY.)

LADY SHOPPER: Excuse me, but are you two in line?

(FRANK *and* LEROY *look at each other, then smile.)*

FRANK: Actually, now that you mention it, Ma'am, I'd say we just got ourselves and our priorities perfectly lined up!

(Blackout.)

The Christmas Feast
(or)
Eat, Drink, and Get Heartburn

A Comedy Sketch

Characters:
DAD
MOM
JIMMY
PAULINE
HARRY

Setting:
The family dining room table with five chairs

Props:
A complete set of dirty dishes (If you don't have access to any, feel free to contact author.)

Costumes:
Modern-day dress

▽

(Sketch opens with everyone sitting at the table. The meal has just been completed. The family is, in a word, stuffed. In fact, they're so full, they can hardly talk.)

DAD: Ohhhhhhhh! I can't believe we ate all that.

MOM: There's one pea left. *(She passes the plate.)*

JIMMY: I'll split it with you.

MOM: Only if you take the larger half.

PAULINE: What a meal! I must have gained 10 pounds!

HARRY: Ten? You ate that much in dressing.

PAULINE: Well, all I can say is I'm glad I'm wearing stretch pants.

JIMMY: Yeah, but will they stretch to Idaho?*

HARRY: I can't even breathe. Meals like this should come with after-dinner oxygen.

DAD: Well, I'm so full, I can't even move.

MOM: You were doing all right a minute ago when you reached for your third helping of mashed potatoes.

DAD: I know, but that was before the four slices of apple pie à la mode.

MOM: À la mode? Is that what you call that mountain of ice cream you had?

DAD: A little scoop. Big deal.

MOM: I've skied down smaller slopes than that!

JIMMY: Well, I know now I never should have finished off that turkey.

MOM: Yeah, especially before the rest of us had a chance to see it.

JIMMY: I left you guys some.

MOM: Ever try splitting a gizzard four ways?

DAD (to MOM): Well, you made quite a dent in the gravy yourself, you know.

MOM: Can I help it if I like gravy?

DAD: So do I, but I don't drink it with a straw.

PAULINE: Well, I'd sure like to know how I ate as much as I did.

HARRY: I'd say it was mostly with your fork. You only used your fingers once, and that seemed to be the easiest way to get 10 olives at one time.

JIMMY: I don't even know what all I ate. I don't remember anything after the centerpiece.

*Idaho residents may insert Florida.

DAD: Well, I don't know about anyone else, but I feel like taking a nap.

HARRY: Me, too. Why is that?

MOM: Why is what?

HARRY: Why is it after a big meal like this you always feel like taking a nap.

JIMMY: Oh, that's easy.

DAD: I guess it's a biological phenomenon, huh?

JIMMY: No, more like simple survival. The first one asleep doesn't have to do the dishes. *(They all immediately pass out.)*

The Birthday Party

A Comedy Sketch

Characters:

LEE
LOUISE
SUNNY
JUDY
GENE
GEORGE
RICK
CHARLENE
RON

Setting:

Stage is decorated for a birthday party—balloons, crepe paper, etc.
There should be a table, chairs and/or sofa.

Props:

A bowl for charade titles; birthday cake (on table); knife for cutting
cake; glasses of punch; forks; paper plates

Costume:

Modern-day dress

▽

(Sketch opens with LEE *standing centerstage, excitely looking over the deco-rations.)*

LEE: Today's the day! MY birthday! And it couldn't happen to a nicer guy!
. . . Now, let's see. . . . The cake's ready, the punch is poured, and the
decorations are all set up. Everything's perfect. All I need now are
my friends. *(A doorbell rings offstage.)* That's probably them now. *(He
walks over to side of stage and opens door. The rest of the cast enters,
carrying beautifully wrapped packages.)* Hi, everybody! *(They walk
right past him.)* Oh, wow, are those my gifts?

LOUISE: No, these are for a little gift exchange we're going to have later. We thought it'd be fun.

LEE (*disappointed*): You mean, none of those are for me?

LOUISE: Of course not, silly. We'll get you something later.

SUNNY: We just didn't have enough time to shop for you. We had all these other gifts to buy.

LEE: Oh, that's all right. The important thing is that you're here.

CHARLENE: Say, would you look at all these decorations!

LEE: You like them?

CHARLENE: Are you kidding? They're fabulous. . . . But they might get in our way when we play games. (*Starts to take down a few streams of crepe paper.*) You don't mind, do you?

LEE: Uh . . . no, I guess not.

GENE: So, what shall we play?

LEE: Well, I thought charades would be . . .

RON: Charades! I'm great at charades!

(LEE *picks up bowl of charade titles.* GEORGE *takes it out of his hand.*)

GEORGE: Now, let's see. Four to a team. Louise, Sunny, Rick, and Ron will be on one team. Judy, Gene, Charlene, and myself will be on the other.

LEE: Hey, what about me?

GEORGE: You don't mind sitting this one out, do you?

LEE: Uh, . . . well, no, I guess not. But you know, it IS my birthday.

RICK: OF COURSE, it's your birthday! That's why we're all here. . . . Now, go stand over there while we play.

(*They begin playing charades off to the side, quietly.*)

LEE (*to himself*): Boy, just look at them. It's MY birthday, and they're the only ones having any fun. They didn't bring me any gifts. They didn't wish me a happy birthday. And now they're acting like I'm not even here.

JUDY (*she laughs then calls out to* LEE *from where they're playing*): Boy, Lee, you sure know how to throw a party. This is great!

LEE (unenthusiastically): I'm glad you're enjoying yourself.

RON: OK, guys, one more round and it's refreshment time.

LEE (to himself): Well, maybe now I'll get some attention.

(GEORGE draws a title from the charade bowl, and starts miming being blown away by a fierce wind.)

SUNNY: Gone with the Wind!

GEORGE: Right!

(Everyone laughs.)

RON: All right, that's it. Cake is served.

(They all walk over and look at the cake.)

GENE: I'll do the honors. (Picks up knife and starts cutting.)

LEE: But what about the candles?

GEORGE: Oh, we don't need to bother. There's enough light in here.

LEE (disappointed): Well, do I at least get the first piece?

GENE (handing RON a piece): Sorry, too late. Who's next?

(Everyone cuts in line in front of LEE until he is at the end of the line. By the time he reaches the front of the line, there's only one piece left.)

LEE: I don't believe it. You mean I actually get a piece of my own birthday cake?

GENE: Sorry, I haven't had mine yet. (GENE takes the last piece himself and starts eating it.) You don't mind, do you?

LEE: No, I guess not.

GENE: What a sport! (Slaps him on the back.)

LEE: But the least you guys could do is sing "Happy Birthday" to me.

RICK: Me? Sing?

SUNNY: I can't sing. I've got a cold.

CHARLENE: Well, I know I didn't take nine years of voice lessons just to sing a round of "Happy Birthday."

GENE: Hey, you guys, there's plenty of punch here.

(They all rush to the table and take the only eight cups. LEE arrives at the table too late again.)

LEE: I'll take a cup.

GENE: Sorry, you're just not quick enough.

RICK: Who's for another game of charades?

JUDY: I'm always ready.

SUNNY: You can count me in, too.

CHARLENE: Me, too.

LEE: Can I play this time?

RON: What do you say we keep the same teams. That way there's less confusion.

GENE: Sounds good to me.

(They walk over to the side of the stage once more and resume playing charades, quietly. RON is acting out a song title. LEE is alone, centerstage.)

LEE *(to himself)*: Boy, what good's a birthday party if your friends are going to forget who it's for?

SUNNY *(involved in the game)*: It's a song? Two words?

LEE *(sarcastically)*: Try "Happy Birthday."

(RON shakes his head.)

GENE: No, that's not it.

LEE: Didn't think so. *(He straightens a few decorations, then softly and solemnly starts singing to himself.)* Happy birthday to me . . . happy birthday to me . . .

RICK *(calls out to LEE)*: Hey, could you please keep it down. We're trying to celebrate your birthday over here!

LEE *(to audience)*: You know, I wonder if this is how Jesus feels sometimes. *(He continues singing slowly.)* Happy birthday . . . happy birthday . . . happy birthday to Me. *(He quietly walks offstage while his friends continue their game of charades.)*

(Blackout.)

A Different Christmas

A Comedy Sketch

Characters:

> DAD
> MOM
> MATT
> JENNIFER
> TOMMY

Setting:

> A living room, complete with sofa, two chairs, tables, Christmas tree, and presents

Props:

> Whistle
> Bible

▽

(Sketch opens with MOM *sitting in one of the chairs.* MATT, JENNIFER, *and* TOMMY *are sitting on the sofa.* DAD *is standing by the tree with the whistle in his hand. The Bible is on a table near the empty chair.)*

DAD: All right, this year we're going to open the gifts in an orderly fashion.

OTHERS *(in unison):* Right. *(They all rush to the gifts and start to raid them.* DAD *blows the whistle. They go back to their seats.)*

DAD: I do not want this to be a repeat of last year.

OTHERS *(in unison):* Right. *(They, again, rush to the tree and start grabbing presents.* DAD *blows the whistle once more. They stop, turn, and look back at him.)*

DAD: I *said* I do *not* want this to be a repeat of last year.

MATT: It's not! The tree's still standing.

DAD: Put the gifts back.

TOMMY: Aw, Dad.

DAD: Put 'em back.

JENNIFER: But . . .

MOM: C'mon. You heard your father.

(They grumble, but finally put the gifts back and take their seats once more.)

DAD: I've decided this Christmas is going to last longer than the 30 seconds it takes to rip the wrapping off all the gifts.

MATT: Well, we could stretch it out to 45 seconds, but that's throwing in all the "thank-yous."

DAD: My point, exactly! Why do we always have to be in such a rush?

MOM: Dear, would you rather us open the presents one at a time?

JENNIFER: The last time we tried that, half our warranties expired before we got to the last gift.

DAD: All I want us to do is take time to remember what this day really means.

MATT: We know what it means. It means we finally get to open our presents! *(To others)* Now, on your mark! *(They prepare to pounce on the gifts again.)* Get set! *(They edge forward in their seats.)* Go! *(They start to go for the gifts again, but DAD blows his whistle. They stop, and settle back in their seats.)*

DAD: Do you think these gifts are all there is?

TOMMY *(excited)*: You mean, you've got MORE presents hid somewhere?!

DAD: I mean, getting presents isn't all there is to Christmas. Christmas is Jesus' birthday. That's what we're celebrating.

MATT: We know that, Dad. But, we just get so excited.

DAD: There's nothing wrong with the excitement over gift-giving, or any of the other festivities. It's just that for once can't we have more than dried pine needles in the carpet and February charge statements to remember Christmas by?

MOM: Your father's right. We're usually in such a hurry to open the gifts and get the turkey on the table, we sing one bar of a Christmas carol and think that's enough.

DAD: But this Christmas is going to be different. The presents will wait, and the turkey can always use a little more time in the oven. *(He sits in the chair, takes the Bible from nearby table, and opens it.)* This year we're inviting Him to the celebration. *(He begins to read.)* "And it came to pass in those days, that there went out a decree from Caesar Augustus, that all the world should be taxed. And all went to be taxed, every one into his own city. And Joseph also went up from Galilee, out of the city of Nazareth, into Judaea, unto the city of David, which is called Bethlehem, . . . to be taxed with Mary his espoused wife, being great with child." *(He hands the Bible to* MOM.*)*

MOM *(continuing the Scripture reading)*: "And so it was, that, while they were there, the days were accomplished that she should be delivered. And she brought forth her firstborn son, and wrapped him in swaddling clothes, and laid him in a manger; because there was no room for them in the inn." *(She hands the Bible to* MATT. *He continues reading.)*

MATT: "And there were in the same country shepherds abiding in the field, keeping watch over their flock by night. And, lo, the angel of the Lord came upon them, and the glory of the Lord shone round about them: and they were sore afraid." *(He hands the Bible to* JENNIFER. *She continues.)*

JENNIFER: "And the angel said unto them, Fear not: for, behold, I bring you good tidings of great joy, which shall be to all people. For unto you is born this day in the city of David a Saviour, which is Christ the Lord." *(She hands the Bible to* TOMMY.*)*

TOMMY *(reading)*: And this shall be a sign unto you; Ye shall find the babe wrapped in swaddling clothes, lying in a manger." *(He hands the Bible back to* DAD.*)*

DAD *(reads)*: "And suddenly there was with the angel a multitude of the heavenly host praising God, and saying, Glory to God in the highest, and on earth peace, good will toward men." *(He reverently closes the Bible, and places it back on the table. He looks up and smiles.)* Now, we can celebrate Christmas.

MOM: Wait, dear. There's just one more thing. (MOM *begins to softly sing "SILENT NIGHT." One at a time, the others join in. At the conclusion of the song,* DAD *walks over to the tree, and starts handing out the gifts.)*

DAD *(to all)*: Merry Christmas!